Book of Change

By

Rayan Parker

Table of Contents

Introduction 1

Understanding Habits And Building A Habit Stack 3

Chapter One Understanding Habits and Goal Settings 4

Chapter Two Breaking a Bad Habit & Replacing With Good Ones 11

Chapter Three Habit Stacking, Its Impact & How to Build Habits Stacking Routine 16

A Collection Of Healthy Habits 26

Chapter Four Good Relationship Habits 27

Chapter Five Healthy Habits 32

Chapter Six The Habits of Highly Spiritual Individuals 37

Chapter Seven Healthy Financial Habits 41

Chapter Eight Essential Daily Organizing Habits 48

Chapter Nine Career Habits 53

Chapter Ten Social Habits that Make you Likable 58

Final Thoughts 64

Sources 65

Introduction

Have you lived with patterns and behaviors that have over the years strengthened? Are you interested in learning how to overcome your unhealthy habits and cultivate new ones? "Cultivate New Habits To Enhance Your Life is a book which explores how you can link your new habits to a cycle that has already been built into your brain and help you stick to the new behavior.

Habits no doubt play a vital role in our daily life and every one of us acquire different habits at some point. Well, habits may be good or bad and they often assert themselves more strongly whenever we are under stress than when we are calm and deliberate.

If you must stay on track toward achieving your goals even in difficult moments, then you need to cultivate new habits which will replace the negative ones. This is the perfect book for anyone looking for the habits of highly successful people in different areas of life.

One of the things that differentiate successful people from unsuccessful people are the habits they have cultivated over the years. Highly successful people around the world have developed positive habits that enable them achieve their goals faster. These habits enable them do things that yield outstanding results even without thinking about them. It involves the small actions they take every day toward their big goals.

Are you ready to explore some positive habits of successful people? Do you genuinely want to replace some of the negative habits you're currently battling with but have no idea how to go about it? Well, this is the right book you should be reading. Get ready to overhaul your old habits and emerge a better and stronger person. Now, let's get started!

Understanding Habits And Building A Habit Stack

Chapter One

Understanding Habits and Goal Settings

Undoubtedly, habits and goals are just two sides of the success coin. While goals provide us with a sense of direction, effective habits offer us the mental discipline to enable us to accomplish our goals. Actually, one without the other usually results in frustration and failure. In the course of forming long-lasting good habits and improving your goal-setting skills, there are some techniques that you can learn.

But what is the Purpose of Goals?

When it comes to developing good habits, goals serve as a focus which helps to identify an ideal end-state for which someone needs to do something to attain the outcome. They are targets that are consciously defined, which helps to give our life context and meaning and also ensures that we remain focused on achieving success. Individuals who live a life that's directed by goals actually direct their activities toward the achievement of something while those without life goals usually fall into a routine and can only "get by" as best as they can.

When it comes to goal setting, majority of experts often suggest that we set SMART goals – specific, measurable, achievable, realistic and time-limited goals. When you say something like I want to lose weight, this doesn't represent an effective goal since there isn't anything that describes what success really looks like. But, saying something like "I'll lose 30 pounds within the next five months" is a goal that's more effective because it can be measured and has a deadline.

Well, saying something like, I want to lose 350 pounds within the next two days," that's definitely not a good goal because it's neither realistic nor achievable.

Habits

> *"All our life, so far as it has definite form, is but a mass of habits"*
> - William James

The second concept we're going to look at is a habit. It has to do with a pattern of behavior which over time turns into someone's default response to a situation. Habits can either be positive or negative. Examples of negative habits include smoking cigarettes, procrastination, alcoholism, dishonesty, lethargy, drug addiction, stealing, and several others. Some examples of positive habits include, writing, regular exercising, reading, meditation, hardworking, etc. The focus of this book is on how to cultivate good habits that will help you live a fulfilled life.

Generally, habitual behaviors often assert themselves more strongly when a person is under stress than when the person is calm and deliberate. This implies that developing good habits and eliminating the negative ones will enable someone to stay on track even during trying times. Habits play an essential role in our daily lives and every one of us have acquired different kinds of habits and they are part of our lives.

Habit Formation

When it comes to habit formation, there are two ways to explain it – psychological and physiological. The psychological theories are of the view that habits are acquired dispositions. So, a learning process or experience which a person gains is retained. As soon as the learning experience is repeated, it will firmly be retained and our ability to retain the learning experience will enable us to get the experience strengthened and it will eventually turn into a habit.

In other words, it's perceived as a link between a stimulus and a response and serves as a mental connection between an event or a trigger thought (stimulus) and our response to the trigger. The repetition of this connection severally will lead to the formation of a habit and this will also affect all subsequent decisions and actions. Also, if repeated sufficiently, this connection will almost become permanent unless we consciously act toward changing it.

The physiological basis has to do with our nervous system. So, when an act is repeated severally, a clear nervous connection will be established and this will lead to a pathway. It leads to smooth shifting of nerve energy, which may be from sensory to motor. Anytime a stimulus is repeated resulting in a response; the connection will, in turn, be strengthened. This will eventually lead to an organization in the nervous system regarded as a habit or in other words, "learning."

So, based on the two perspectives, we can conclude that a habit works through the habit loop:

- **A Trigger/Cue** - A location, certain people, an emotional state and a time of day.
- **It involves a Routine** - Smoking cigarette, biting your nails, exercising, healthy snacking, eating chocolate, watching TV, etc.
- **A Reward** - This has to do with the pleasure chemicals that are released in the brain as a result of the routine and because of the reward, the habit is reinforced.

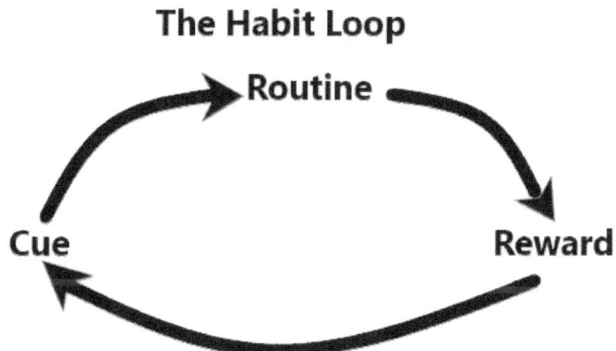

A look at the loop above reveals that it is actually a self-reinforcing mechanism which with time will become automatic. It's interesting to note that once a habit emerges, then the brain will instantly stop participating "fully" in decision making. Once you're able to understand how habit works via the habit loop, then it becomes quite easier for you to take control of your habits. So, it's possible to change the "logic of the loop," by breaking a habit down into its components earlier mentioned.

Having the Right Habits

The reason why we don't need to relearn everything we do is that habits are encoded in the structures of the human brain which actually saves us a lot of effort needed to relearn things we've learned before. This automation of our actions frees up energy, which we can use in focusing on other tasks. While this works to our advantage, it also enables us to form negative habits. In case a bad habit is created, then one way to change it is by interrupting it first before installing a new one.

Unless you consciously work toward eliminating a bad habit and replacing it with new routines through habit stacking as we shall see later, the negative patterns will unfold automatically and repeatedly whenever the habit is activated by the trigger. Our brain doesn't have what it takes to differentiate between good and bad habits, so you need to do that. You have to intentionally decide what actions/routines you want to have and then leverage the habit loop.

To create positive changes for yourself, all you have to do is to turn your desired actions into habits. Always bear in mind that all habits can be ignored, changed or totally replaced though this isn't very easy because habits don't entirely disappear – they can only be replaced by new habits. It's impossible to cause your habits to disappear – the best you can do is to change it – and this can be achieved by using the Golden Rule:

• Make use of the same cue/trigger

- Modify the routine
- Provide the same reward

Types of Habit

There are several categories of habit and it's usually easy to identify bad habits in other people around you; however, you don't have to be lured into learning from such observations since the ones that really count are the ones you discover in yourself. Let's see some categories of habits:

✓ **Strategy habits -** This refers to how we solve problems or deal with situations. While some of these strategies favor us; like planning, others may not really work very well for us – like working on things in the last minute.

✓ **Relationship habits -** They are the habits that we form based on how we interact with other people, such as showing off, forgiving, showing kindness, aggressive, and being considerate.

✓ **Thinking habits -** The habits that fall under this category include reactions, prejudices, attitudes and biases. For instance, "all women like shopping."

✓ **Timing habits -** They are related to the habits that involve time management such as managing deadlines, prioritizing, estimating, and delegating.

✓ **Emotional habits -** This involves habits that trigger emotions such as being afraid while in an abusive relationship or having a relaxed feeling anytime you're taking a bath.

- ✓ **Ego habits -** These include habits that are connected to territory, power and status. For instance, insisting that you must be addressed in a particular way by someone else just to prove that you're powerful or influential.
- ✓ **Physical habits -** The physical habits have to do with moving and making use of your body which includes the way you laugh, stand, speak, laugh, etc.

This is just a brief introduction of the categories of habits; we shall take a deeper look at some of these habits to help you develop more positive habits.

Chapter Two

Breaking a Bad Habit & Replacing
With Good Ones

"We are what we repeatedly do. Excellence then, is not an act, but a habit."

— Will Durant

There are several disadvantages of having bad habits; they hinder you from accomplishing your goals, waste your time and energy, and even affect your health physically and mentally. I'm sure the main reason why you picked up this book is to cultivate good habits and if you must have good habits, then you need to replace the bad ones you're having right now. Well, before we talk about how to replace your bad habits with good ones, let's understand the main causes of bad habits.

Causes of Bad Habits

Basically, it's been discovered that there are two things that lead to bad habits and they are stress and boredom! In most cases, you will discover that your bad habits are just your way of dealing with stress and boredom. Whether it's overspending on a shopping spree, biting your nails, spending so much time on the internet and social media, drinking every weekend, etc., they are all forms of response to stress and boredom.

Well, it doesn't have to be that way; it's possible to learn healthy ways to deal with stress and boredom and then substitute the bad ones with the good ones. This does not imply that there are no other causes apart from stress and boredom – they could be as a result of deeper issues in your life. Some of these issues could be tough to even think about. If you're genuinely interested in changing the situation, then you must be honest with yourself. Ask yourself right now;

Are there other reasons or beliefs behind your bad habits?

Is there something deeper than the surface like an event, fear or a limiting belief that has caused you to embrace bad habits?

Being able to identify the main causes of your bad habits is essential to overcoming them. Remember, you don't eliminate habits; you only replace them. In some ways, the bad habits in your life right now provide benefits to you even though they may affect you negatively in other ways.

The benefits are sometimes beneficial for you biologically, like drugs and smoking. Also, it could be emotional benefits like staying in an abusive relationship. It could be your simple way of coping with stress like biting your nails, tapping your foot, clenching your jaw, pulling your hair, etc. Interestingly, these "benefits" or justifications for bad habits often extend to smaller bad habits too. One of the reasons why bad habits are difficult to eliminate is because they provide you with some kind of benefits.

This explains why a simple advice of "stop doing it" just doesn't work. The best way to stop bad habits is to replace them with new and positive habits that offer a similar benefit. So, if you smoke, for instance, ceasing from smoking abruptly whenever you're stressed may not be the best idea. Instead, you can adopt various ways and new habits to help you handle your stress. Bad habits generally address specific needs in our lives, so replacing them with healthier ones that address the same needs is your best option for dealing with bad habits.

Tips for Breaking a Bad habit

Now that you know that the best way to break a bad habit is by replacing it, let's look at other tips to help you get rid of your bad habits.

1. Identify a substitute for your bad habit

It's crucial to plan on how to deal with stress and boredom when it comes since that's what prompts the bad habit. So, when you get the urge to smoke, what are you going to do? Go ahead and choose various options like breathing exercises instead of smoking. If you discover that Facebook is inviting you to procrastinate, you can write a sentence for work. The idea is to have a plan for what you'll do instead of a bad habit.

2. As much as possible, eliminate your triggers

Do you always smoke whenever you drink? Well, simply don't go to the bar. Are you fond of eating those unhealthy snacks whenever you're home? Go ahead and throw them all away or replace them with healthy snacks like fruits, nuts and vegetables. Find ways to make it easier for you to break your bad habits by completely avoiding their causes. Understand that your environment actually makes it harder for you to embrace good habit and easier to adopt the bad ones.

3. Stay around people with the kind of habits you desire

Although you don't have to ditch your old friends, you need to understand that finding new ones will help you significantly. So, find people with good habits you desire and stay around them.

4. Plan for Failure

"When you screw up, skip a workout, eat bad foods, or sleep in, it doesn't make you a bad person. It makes you human. Welcome to the club."
- Steve Kamb

The truth is that you will definitely slip at some point. But instead of beating yourself up because of a mistake, plan for it. What really separates top performers from others is that whenever they get off track, they always get back on track fast. So, when you slip, just focus on your goal and try again.

If you're really interested in eliminating bad habits, then you need to start with awareness. You can easily get carried away with how you feel regarding the bad habits and end up feeling very guilty. You end up spending much time wishing that things were better. Unfortunately, these thoughts take you gradually away from the real things happening in your life right now. What you need is awareness because that's how you can truly make a change. So ask yourself these questions:

- How many times do I engage in this habit each day?
- When does your bad habit often happen?
- Who are you with?
- Where are you?
- What are the triggers that cause the bad habit to start?

When you successfully track these issues, you will become more conscious and enlightened about the behavior. Then you can start coming up with several ideas for stopping them. Just go ahead and track the number of times your bad habit happens each day. Have a pen and paper ready and mark it down whenever the habit happens. At the end of the day, take count of the number of times it happened.

Your goal at the beginning is not to judge yourself or become guilty about unproductive or unhealthy habits. Instead, focus first on being aware of when it happens and how often it happens. This is how you have a better understanding of the problem before the next step, which is to implement the ideas already talked about in helping you to break the bad habit. Always remember that breaking a bad habit takes time and effort, so you need to be patient.

A good number of people who successfully break bad habits tried and failed several times before they finally got it right. Although you might still be struggling right now, it doesn't mean that you can't change the habit, just keep working on it.

Chapter Three

Habit Stacking, Its Impact & How to Build Habits Stacking Routine

"Motivation is what gets you started. Habit is what keeps you going."

— Jim Ryun

Undoubtedly, remarkable changes often come in small actions. However, the challenge is how to add a series of small changes to a simple-to-do framework and that's where habit stacking comes in. So, what is habit stacking? Although the term might appear complex, it's quite straightforward. It involves linking actions together to create a routine – there are multiple mini-habits in each routine. The new habits don't have to be lengthy actions; they are a series of small changes that you can link together to create a ritual that you follow each day.

It is also known as "habit chaining," it has to do with the process of categorizing small activities into a routine and linking them to a habit which you set in a day. This is what makes the routine you create memorable and successfully anchors the new habits you formed to an existing trigger – using specific things you always remember to remind yourself to do other things.

Why Is Habit Stacking Effective?

According to an Oxford University research which took place in 2007, it was discovered that the average adult human actually had just 41 percent fewer neurons in the brain compared to newborn babies. Well, this does not imply that adults are more stupid than a baby; instead, it implies that adults pass through a process known as synapse pruning. In the words of a behavioral psychologist James Clear:

"Your brain prunes away connections between neurons that don't get used and builds up connections that get used more frequently."

The process of synaptic pruning takes place with every single habit we build – since the brain actually builds a strong network of neurons to support your existing behaviors. So, the more you engage in an action, the stronger and also more efficient the connections will become. This implies that you need to take advantage of all the strong habits and connections that you don't take seriously each day to build new and positive habits.

Another major reason why habit stacking works is that it enables you to break down bigger problems into smaller actions which you can easily handle. Also, since you connect all the actions, it's quite easy to remember to execute the tasks and reinforce them. With habit stacking, you can easily eliminate the stress of attempting to change so many things at the same time. Your main objective is to mainly focus on a single routine at a time which doesn't require more than 15 or 20 minutes to execute.

Well, within a single routine, you will have several actions (or you can call them small changes). Basically, all you need to do is to create a checklist which you will follow during the day.

Hopefully, you should have gained a better understanding of what habit stacking means. But, it's undoubtedly not an easy task to add multiple new habits to your day; however, it's fairly easy to build a single new routine. Let's focus on some steps you will take to turn small positive habits into a simple-to-complete sequence which you can use daily. The main idea is that rather than treat a habit stack like a series of individual tasks, you need to handle a habit stack just like a single action.

This might initially appear as a simple task, but the truth is that it requires several elements. It will be very overwhelming for you to treat each component of a stack as an individual action because you will need to create a reminder for each task and also keep track of every behavior. On the other hand, you can make things easier to remember and also complete each day by treating the entire routine as a single habit.

At first, habit stacking can seem overwhelming, but as soon as you start and act on it a few times, then it would no longer appear as hard as you thought initially. If you must succeed with habit stacking, then you have to start with small expectations which will enable you to build the muscle memory needed for completing this routine and as soon as you're consistent, you can even add more tasks. So, let's go through some of the steps required to create long-lasting positive change in your life.

1. First, Begin with a Five-Minute Block

You can easily adhere to a new habit by making it "stupidly simple" to accomplish. For instance, if you want to write on a daily basis and create a book, then simply break it down; write just one paragraph each day. Although you can easily do more, once you write your daily one-paragraph target, you will regard the task as being completed for the day. This, however, will help you achieve your goal and at the same time, set simple goals that overcome inertia. In fact, as soon as you've started, you will end up doing more tasks than you initially planned. The main point here is consistency; begin with five minutes, selecting two or three habits and continue to add more when this routine turns into automatic actions.

2. Take note of Small Wins

When you focus on small wins, you can easily build emotional momentum since you can easily remember and complete them. So, start by building your routine around habits which doesn't require much of effort to complete. These are actions that require little willpower, such as reviewing your goals or weighing yourself. By starting with no-brainer tasks, you will eliminate the chances of skipping an activity each day because of the feeling of being overwhelmed or too busy. You only can add more habits to your routine after focusing on these simple activities for a week or more until it's automatic.

3. Choose a Time and Location

You need to anchor every stack to a trigger which is related to a time of day, location or both.

4. Your Habit Stack should be anchored to a Trigger

Remember we talked about the habit loop earlier and one of the things needed to perform a habit is a trigger. Trigger here has to do with a cue that makes use of at least one of your five senses to serve as a reminder to complete a particular action. The reason why triggers are crucial is that people often find it difficult to remember a large collection of tasks without using a reminder. But, a trigger can cause you to take action. This explains why some people use alarm clocks or cell phones to wake themselves up in the morning. Basically, there are two types of trigger;

- **Internal triggers -** These are feelings, emotions and thoughts that have to do with an established habit.
- The second one is an external trigger such as a push notification, phone alarm, or even the post-it note placed on a refrigerator. They help lead to a reaction once an alarm goes off and you proceed to complete the task.

Understanding the two types of trigger will not just enable you to build powerful habit stacks, but will also enable you to overcome bad habits that might actually be affecting your personal development and growth.

5. Come up with a Logical Checklist

Actually, the most crucial aspect of a stack is the checklist which needs to include a sequence of actions, where you will do them and how long it will take to handle each task. Although it might be a bit obsessive to add all this information, it will help you eliminate guesswork regarding the things you need to do to complete a particular action. Don't forget to add the small actions together so that they would seamlessly flow into each other without stress.

6. You should be Accountable

"An object at rest stays at rest and an object in motion stays in motion with the same speed and in the same direction unless acted upon by an unbalanced force."
- The Law of Inertia

This implies that if your natural tendency is to lounge around before you start your day, then what you need to force yourself into action is an extra "push." One of the reasons why people fail while building habits is that it's much easier to remain resting than it is to engage in something new and likely unpleasant. In fact, you need accountability to stick to a major goal.

Making a personal commitment isn't enough. To accomplish something big in life, you need a solid action plan as well as a support network to be there for you in case you experience an obstacle. You can be accountable in several ways, like informing your close friends about your new routine, spelling out punishments for yourself for not being committed to your goals using apps such as **Beeminder** or by posting your progress on your social media accounts.

7. Have Small and Enjoyable Rewards

Understand that it's an accomplishment to complete your habit stacking routine. One significant motivator for completing a daily routine is to give yourself a reward. Examples of such rewards include eating a healthy snack, relaxing for a few minutes or watching your favorite TV show. Apart from these, a reward can also be anything that you often enjoy, but make sure that you avoid any reward that tends to eliminate the benefit of having a particular habit. For instance, if you're interested in losing weight and have just completed small actions that will help you achieve it, you shouldn't reward yourself with something like a 400-calorie cupcake. This will not help you in your weight loss efforts.

8. Focus on Repetition

Within the first few weeks of building a habit stack, your main focus should be on repetition. It's crucial to stick to the routine when you miss out on small actions. Consistency is the most crucial aspect of building a stack because one way to build muscle memory is by repetition.

Once you're able to complete the routine frequently enough, then it will turn into an ingrained part of your day like taking your bath. Don't forget that it's not also the end of the world when you miss the occasional day, but avoid missing two days in a row. If you do, it will progressively make it easier for you to miss future days.

9. Avoid Breaking the Chain

The main goal of not breaking the chain is to remove all excuses. In fact, it's sometimes easy to think of creative reasons why you shouldn't get started with a stack. There would be lots of excuses: hangover, depressed, tired, overwhelmed, sick or even busy. These excuses will make it easy for you to skip a routine.

Once you regularly miss a day, it will then become easier to skip another day anytime you don't feel like doing something on the list. The best way to avoid breaking the chain is to create a doable daily goal which you can easily achieve regardless of what happens. Also, don't let yourself to be talked out of it.

10. Be Prepared to Face Setbacks

Actually, you can experience occasional setbacks or challenges with the most consistent habits. Even when you've done something for a long time, be assured that at some point, you may also experience unexpected setbacks. But setbacks help us to realize the importance of resilience and adhering to something even while experiencing a setback. So, expect challenges once you embark on your routine and when they appear, you have the chance to either give up or search for ways to overcome them.

11. Have a Schedule for the Frequency of a Stack

It's possible to complete some stacks on an irregular basis such as daily, weekly or even monthly. When starting, you can focus on small daily habit stack, but once you're comfortable with the strategy, then you need to create a stack for every time frame earlier mentioned. When you put them into a routinely scheduled activity, you will ensure that the tasks are completed without disturbing your subconscious as a project that you are yet to complete.

12. Your Stack should be Scaled up

Remember the first step we talked about in this process – starting with a five-minute block. Well, you won't get much value from habit stacking if all you do is to devote limited time to a stack. So, to build positive habits, you need to later build up to at least thirty minutes routine and complete at least six small habits. You can accomplish this in an incremental manner; for instance, during the first week, the duration of your routine should be five minutes.

Then scale it up to ten minutes in the second week, fifteen minutes in week three, then repeat the entire process until you get to thirty minutes with several actions. You don't have to add a bunch of small habits, rather, ensure that you're consistently finishing the routine without resistance to this activity. When it comes to your stack, you don't have to ignore your feelings of boredom and stress.

Once you start noticing that it's getting progressively difficult to start and you're procrastinating, then you can either ask yourself why you want to skip a day or reduce the number of habits. It will be easier to overcome your lack of motivation by understanding why you're not motivated in the first place.

13. Create One Routine Per Time

How long it takes to build a permanent habit remains one of the biggest debates around. While some are of the view that it should be 21 days, others believe that it's only for a few months. Don't try to build more than a habit at a time since every new action will also make it more difficult to stick to your stacks. One easy way to add a new stack is when you no longer think of a habit as a habit.

A Collection Of Healthy Habits

Chapter Four

Good Relationship Habits

When it comes to having a happy relationship, then, you should bear in mind that habits have an outstanding impact on it. They can either make your relationship healthy and happy or even destroy your relationships. Our focus right now is on healthy and positive habits that will boost your relationship. The foundation of every positive relationship are positive habits; they create and also maintain healthy and strong relationships.

The foundation of every positive relationship are positive habits and once bad habits are present, it affects the relationship negatively. So, what are some of these positive habits that make relationships healthy and strong?

1. Respecting Each Other

One of the most crucial habits of positive relationships is respect and the reason for this is that it fosters trust and acceptance. One easy way to slowly weaken trust and create barriers in connection with each other is to show disrespect toward your partner. Most times, disagreements lead to arguments which in turn leads to insults. So, ensure that you monitor what you say – think before uttering a word which could result in negative consequences.

2. Always Respond to Each other

Available statistics reveal that about 86 percent of couples who are happily married respond to their partner's bid for attention. On the other hand, only 30 percent of couples who are unhappy do the same. One of the best ways to show your attention is by responding to your partner anytime you're asked a question. Learn to bring something home whenever you're coming home from work. It's all about showing your responsiveness and attentiveness whenever something occurs.

3. Always stay Connected All Through the Day

Right from the moment we wake up in the morning to the time we retire to our beds at night, we are always busy. Well, you're almost no different too. But showing love and affection when couples apart, play a crucial role in having a long and happy relationship. Once you make a commitment to someone, you essentially place the person top on the list of your priorities in life. You shouldn't allow anything to affect that commitment, not even your hectic work schedule. Endeavor to connect with each other all through the day by calling your partner on your way home or sending a text during your break.

4. Avoid Distractions When you're with your Partner

We don't always have sufficient time with each other as it's supposed to be especially with our work and obligations. If you continue to allow distractions to interrupt your time alone, then you may be causing serious damage to your relationship and this will, in turn, affect your intimacy with your partner.

In most cases, preoccupation with work is the greatest distraction which affects couples trying to get closer. So, you need to develop the habit of eliminating distractions when you're with your partner. Turn off the TV, keep your phones when you're spending time alone and always ensure that office work remains completed before you come home.

5. Habit of Forgiving

Every one of us has personal flaws, so, you can't find someone that's perfect. What you need is to find someone who is "perfect for you." With time, you will begin to discover that the person you fell in love with has some flaws that push your buttons. You need to imbibe the habit of accepting the shortcomings of your partner, forgive and love your partner. This is indeed one of the ways to ensure that your relationship is a healthy one.

6. The habit of Surprising your Partner

It's usually natural to reach a point in your relationship where the feelings of infatuation and intrigue with the other begins to weaken. But what you need to avoid at this point is complacency as well as the feelings of complacency. When it comes to relationships, spontaneity is fun and healthy; it results in the feelings of appreciation and love. Even though these spontaneous gestures are big or small, always ensure that it's clear you made efforts to do something special for your partner. You may not be the creative type and that's okay. You can take advantage of excellent ideas on the internet.

7. Learn to take some time Apart

The first question that readily comes to your mind is; how can I stay connected to my partner while taking time apart? Well, that's a great question. Time apart can be very healthy and productive when frustrations occur in a relationship. One of the things that healthy couples recognize is the importance of taking time apart. This helps to deepen the appreciation and love for each other. It also provides them with a quiet time. This can be in the form of having dinner with friends, going to a movie alone or even watching the television by yourself.

8. Recognize and Appreciate Qualities

One of the must-have habits is conveying positive qualities toward your partner. This doesn't just deepen the emotional connection you have with your partner; it also makes them feel genuinely good about such compliments. So, learn to show admiration and appreciation of the positive attributes of your partner because it will strengthen the bond that currently exists between you and your partner. Constantly bringing someone's shortcomings will end up damaging the relationship and sometimes irreparably damaged.

9. Learn to Find Humor in other's Mistakes

Although relationships are meant to be serious, it shouldn't be serious all the time, especially when a partner makes mistakes. When going into a relationship, you were aware that the other person might likely do something dumb at some point. All you just need to do is to find ways to laugh about it together with your partner.

10. Show Frequent Affection

Records from research indicate that individuals in healthy relationships are abundantly affectionate toward each other. The reason why affection and being close to each other is vital to every relationship is that it increases connection and trust. When you have a healthy level of affection, it strengthens your bond and will create a stronger connection with your partner.

Chapter Five
Healthy Habits

If truly you want to maintain your health, then it's crucial that you embrace healthy habits that you repeatedly do to achieve your goals. For instance, you may end up getting a boost of endorphins after running a half-marathon or an injury. Well, you can also go for a 30 minutes walk or jogging several times each week (all through the year) and experience miracles in the quality of your life and health. So, this section is focused mainly on healthy habits that can significantly improve your physical and mental well-being.

Remember, we talked about habit stacking, so what you need to do to add a habit to your stack is to first pick one and wait until the habit is fully integrated into your daily routine, then go ahead and select another one.

Moving Habits

Some habits you can choose from here include:

✓ **Walking -** As much as possible, try walking when the opportunity comes; going to get some fresh air during your lunch break, shopping, or sightseeing in a new city, make sure you walk. Ideally, the minimum number of steps you need to take every day is 10,000. Although this might seem to be too much, however, every step counts and gets you closer to achieving your target. The best way to cultivate this habit is to see it like a game.

✓ **Regularly stand** - Actually, in some parts of the world, prolonged inactivity is a prevalent issue which is regarded as lack of exercise. Sitting for long hours at a time actually compromises your body's ability to burn fats and sugar which you eat every day. This will, in turn, lead to different health problems. Fortunately, one of the best solutions to this issue is to simply stand up as frequently as possible. Get up from your chair, walk to your coworker's office; use the stairs instead of the elevator, stand up whenever you're making a call. Take advantage of every opportunity you have to stand up and be active each day.

✓ **Straighten your posture** - Things have become easier now for us with the introduction of smartphones. Now, it's possible to set up regular reminders to straighten your posture. At regular intervals, bring your neck and hips to a neutral position, then proceed to pull your shoulder blades back while sticking your chest out. One of the benefits of having a good posture is that it enables all the muscles to work optimally and further reduces pressure on your joints. In addition, it even helps to reduce your risk of experiencing backaches, it energizes you, helps you breathe better and makes you feel more confident.

✓ **Stretch** - Stretching is very important for your health; you don't have to stretch for one hour. Just by moving your body in different ways for a few minutes can help improve your flexibility. It will improve the flexibility of your joints and lower the risk of having an injury. All that's required is to stretch for a few minutes and then you can enjoy several benefits. In fact, due to the influx of oxygenated blood which is sent to your muscles and brain, you will get an instant boost of energy.

Food Habits

Apart from engaging in physical activities, another category of habits that you need to cultivate has to do with the kind of food you eat.

✓ **Embrace fruits** - Although many people know that it's a smart idea to fill half our plates with vegetables and fruits, few of us adhere to it. Whenever you plan your menu, endeavor to add healthy foods like raw vegetables, gratins, purees, smoothies, fresh fruit, salads, stews, and sautés. The ideal ingredients to a healthy diet are fruits and vegetables because they are affordable, packed with nutrients and are low in calories.

✓ **Eat in good company** - Endeavor to connect with real humans, especially during conversations. Conversations are not only meant to help reinforce social bonds; they also make us eat more slowly. It's easy to set your fork down once you feel full but not too full.

✓ **Observe when you feel hungry and full** - One question you need to ask yourself right now is; "How much food should you eat every day? The best answer to this question varies significantly depending on factors such as weight, age, level of physical activity, and gender. One of the best ways to ensure that you're eating sufficiently is to observe your hunger signals. When you discover that your stomach is growling, go ahead and eat and once you feel full, then stop. Stop eating once you feel full even though your plate is not yet empty or someone is offering you extra plate of food.

✓ **Drink water** - If you want to stay hydrated, then you need to stay hydrated. When you're hydrated, you avoid having headaches, fatigue or issues focusing. You can remind yourself regularly to drink water by keeping a reusable bottle on hand and on sight where you can easily see it. Other good options include unsweetened coffee, herbal tea and tea.

✓ **Cook your food** - You can enhance your health by cooking your meal. Take some time during the week to prepare simple, tasty dishes which will save you time during busy days. You don't need much time to cook your food; two hours is all you need to prepare a great meal.

Well-Being Habits

✓ **Breathe** - At frequent intervals, spend some time taking deep breaths. Considering the busy life we're living and the level of stress we're exposed to every day, you may end up taking short and shallow breaths. So, when you spend a few moments breathing deeply, it will help you calm your mind in addition to other physical benefits. It helps to lower your blood pressure as well as heart rate. It can also help in managing your stress.

✓ **Sleep** - This is one of the pillars of good health, just like exercise and a healthy diet. You will enjoy several health benefits which will influence your mood, memory, longevity, physical and cognitive performance positively by simply having enough sleep. Ideally, you need between seven and eight hours of sleep every night; this varies based on age and other factors.

✓ **Endeavor to smile -** Smiling is one of the easiest habits that you can adopt which can significantly affect your mood positively. By just raising the corners of your mouth, your body will produce endorphins which provides you instant happiness.

Chapter Six

The Habits of Highly Spiritual Individuals

Well, we may not be able to discuss the habits of highly spiritual people exhaustively, but we shall focus on some of the most important ones. When you embrace these habits, you will certainly enjoy the benefits such as loving other people, being loved by others and even loving yourself. With time, these habits will become addictive and further lead to various random acts of spiritual goodness which will take over your life and make you a better person. So, let's find out some of these habits.

Highly Spiritual people Give

They are often eager to give instead of taking. Giving is indeed divine; in fact, there are indications from research on altruism which imply that individuals commit to selfless deeds mainly because such acts make them feel good. Giving is undoubtedly human nature and can take various forms – it's actually a gift to pay attention to someone.

Always See Possibilities and not Problems

> *"In the beginner's mind there are many possibilities; in*
> *the expert's mind there are few."*
> - Shunryu Suzuki

A closer look at highly spiritual people will reveal that they are optimists – they are people who believe in belief! They always see problems as opportunities and are advocates of the power of positive thinking.

Often say "Yes" more than "No!"

One of the things that "no" does to us is that it closes our hearts just like cholesterol. Well, this naturally excludes some kind of no such as saying "No" to drugs, illegal and self-destructive behaviors. Generally, people would rather hear yes than no and "yes" affirms life. As much as possible, make your yes more than your no.

Highly Spiritual People Take note of the Blessings in Small wonders

They are not people who expect a supernatural being to appear accompanied by brimstone and fire or a massive neon sign in the sky. These are people who are not waiting for an extraordinary thing to happen before seeing the wonders in them like a spectacular job promotion, meeting the love of a lifetime in a very romantic way, etc.

These are people who appreciate the small details of our everyday life like the first sunlight rays of the morning, the sparkle in the eyes of an older adult or the innocent and charming smile of a child. They appreciate the good small stuff we see every day.

They are Generous with Compliments and Also humbly Accept them

We have an unending need for praise and appreciation and we yearn for it every day in our interactions. Highly spiritual people don't perceive the need for support by others as a flaw or sign of weakness. Instead, they see it as a cry for love and also they don't hesitate to comply. Well, there are others who actually respond to compliment with grandiose objections and deflections and they often don't accept compliments gracefully. Maybe they feel that they don't deserve it even when they do.

Embrace Laughter

Spiritual people are happy; Santa ho-ho-ho, the Laughing Buddha, the Dalai Lama often giggles his way to enlightenment and several others. These people are not just happy facially; they are happy deep down. The act of smiling can lead to a happy hormonal shift – changing from a gloomy mask of tragedy, to the spread of sunshine everywhere.

Always Worship when and where the Spirit Moves you

You don't need to be in a church or temple to practice spirituality and neither do you need a special day as well. In fact, you don't also need a rabbi, a sensei, lama or a priest. In most cases, the ideal spiritual setting includes a mountain top, a beach or forest. So, this implies that the ideal setting is a movable spiritual feast since true spiritual setting lies within. It travels with us and within us everywhere we go.

Show Empathy

Another positive spiritual habit is the act of showing empathy. You should learn to feel the pains of others but not so much to take the pain of others and become another's pain. When you empathize, you can easily know what to say or do to make others feel better.

Chapter Seven
Healthy Financial Habits

Regardless of what your goal may be; financial freedom, to become a millionaire, increase your savings or become debt-free, they all require one thing and that's having good financial habits. We all desire to be financially stable; however, we cannot attain financial stability without having a plan to get there. This section will focus on several financial habits that will help you attain your financial goals.

1. Live within your means

This is perhaps the foundation of all good financial habits. It would be a waste of time for you to set financial goals unless you can live within your means. So, if your monthly income is $7,000 monthly, then simply make sure that you live on $6,000 and bank the rest. Your financial situation will drastically improve as your savings and investments grow.

2. You deserve to Pay yourself

One of the simplest ways to automate the process of saving money is by having a 401K or other employer retirement account. It will help you also to live beneath your means. Always allocate a specific percentage or dollar amount from your pay even before you see or handle it. The money will be moved to your savings and investment accounts without you even noticing it and with time, it will turn into real money. Some of the ways to automate your savings include:

- ✓ Utilizing a cash-backed credit card
- ✓ Setting up automatic monthly transfers
- ✓ Making regular savings deposits
- ✓ Portion your direct-deposit (also revenue streams) into separate savings
- ✓ Saving your tax refund

3. Always buy Value

This implies that you should neither purchase the cheapest items in the market nor the most expensive ones. Rather, search for the items that have the best value for your money and buy them. Although you might need to add extra dough for a product that you know will last, it's better than purchasing an item for the lowest price and always replacing it. Don't forget that not all products are better just because they are more expensive – in most cases, it's just perception and brand. Shop around and read reviews.

4. Always pay your Bills Ahead of time

Whenever you pay your bills late, it only helps to stretch the paycheck. However, it's simply robbing Peter to pay Paul. It simply gives you a false sense of how much money you're having and ends up putting you under immense pressure to balance the difference later. When you pay your bills ahead of time, it will help you gain more control over your finances and also enable you embrace good financial habits.

5. You Simply Can't Afford it if you have to Borrow

Although borrowing to buy a home makes sense since very few people have over $150,000 with which to purchase a home. However, if you must adopt good financial habits, then you need to avoid schemes that end up stretching your paycheck. The most common way to do this is by using credit cards.

6. Make sure you enjoy Consistent Raise

You can easily achieve your financial goals by building progress into your savings and investment funding. One of the best ways to do this is by gradually increasing your payroll savings every year. This is possible by painlessly increasing the savings payroll deduction by just one percentage point each year. It could be for your retirement or other investment or savings account. If you desire to retire early, then the best is to save at least 20 percent of your income. If you want to retire even earlier, then dare to save over 50 percent of your income.

7. Reduce your TV Watching Time

Are you wondering whether watching the television has anything to do with being financially stable? Well, I guess you've forgotten that the TV is an advertising venue. You will discover that apart from commercials, TV shows also have adverts for certain wares via something known as product placement. This is where sponsors of TV shows place their wares and they usually make you feel insecure just because you're not buying what they're selling.

A large percentage of our spending (especially impulse spending), is motivated by the time we spent watching the television. This implies that the less time you spend watching it and the ads that flood your screen, the less money you will be driven to spend on items you don't even need. Don't also forget that when you watch less TV, you can spend that time reading good books that will improve your life.

8. Read Books on Finance

If you're genuinely interested in becoming financially free, then you need to get the advice from financial masters. Leverage the knowledge of financial masters and you can get bankable ideas from just reading a single book and lots more when you read several others.

9. Learn to Shop without Credit Cards

Apart from preventing you from running up your credit card balances, when you make purchases with your credit or debit card, it increases the chances of spending less money that you would have if you're shopping with a credit card. The reason is that you're likely going to make better and wiser decision in the checkout line when you're using real money.

10. Monitor Your spending

I would advise that you create a budget for your home. If you don't have a budget, then you don't also have an idea of how you're spending your money. Interestingly, this is one of the best financial habits that you must adopt if you truly desire to be financially stable. When you have a budget, you will be able to track your spending and identify the areas of excess. When you identify those areas, you will be able to cut back on your expenses in the identified areas. So, have a budget and begin to monitor your spending right now and you'll be amazed to discover where your funds are really going.

11. Always Pay more than the Minimum on your Credit Cards

You need to get rid of those balances on your credit card if you want to take control of your finances. So, if you've not been able to pay off your credit cards before, then endeavor to pay more than the minimum payment due. In addition, consider consolidating your credit card debt under a single zero balance transfer card. The moment you do this, then all high-interest cards will be under a zero-interest card and save you money. Monitor your credit card statements since they will inform you of how long it will take to pay off your balance if you only pay the minimum payment and also how long if you pay a fixed amount which is a bit higher than the minimum payment. In most cases, the difference is for several years.

12. Learn to Say "No" to Your Kids

It's crucial that you learn to say no to your children if you have kids. Kids will always be kids – always demanding something from you. Well, what they demand tends to be more expensive as they become older. So, by learning to say no to random items they see and feel they can't live without, you can save a lot of money.

Well, don't get me wrong here, I'm not advocating that you don't give your children gifts on their birthdays, Christmas, or even things they genuinely need. What I mean is you responding to their impulse buying – always seeing something they like and wanting to have it – but instead of buying it with their money, they are using your money. When you learn to say "no" to their impulse buying, you will have more money in your pocket.

There is also another aspect that you should take seriously; the way you spend money on your children has crucial implications for the attitude your kids will have toward money when they become teenagers and adults. Although it's not always easy to say "no" to your children, especially when they look at you with love, it will teach them an important financial lesson in life. Your kids will learn that it's not possible to have all the candy in the store and this will help them as they prepare for their adult life.

13. Learn to Say "No" to Yourself

Apart from your kids, you should also learn to say no to yourself, especially when you are shopping or going for a walk. This has to do with controlling your impulse buying. You often find yourself tempted to buy something you like while walking past a shop and you end up buying it simply because you feel it doesn't cost much. Well, this has even become easier than it was before because you can buy anything you like online and it will be delivered to your doorstep. When you do this several times each week, you will soon find out that your spending has started adding up.

One strategy you should adopt is the "72-hour rule" on all your purchases, especially when shopping online. After choosing the items you want to buy, add them to your shopping cart and wait for 72 hours before finally buying the items. Within this time, you should be convinced whether you truly need the item or not.

14. Learn to Give to Others

This could be cooking a meal for a friend who is in need, donating your money or time to a charity cause, tithing, etc. The point here is putting the needs of others before yours. Although focusing on your worries and concerns is often the easiest thing to do, when you focus on others, the payback is usually immeasurable.

Chapter Eight
Essential Daily Organizing Habits

Undoubtedly, the primary reason why we usually feel overwhelmed in our daily life is that we allow the small things in our home to pile up instead of working on them at the moment. The cycle is always an interesting one – the main reason why we fail to deal with some tasks is that we feel it would take away valuable time that we would use for other things we feel are more valuable. But we usually end up being compelled to spend more time working on those things once they have reached a limit which we can no longer ignore.

It's often a time-consuming activity to reorganize something that has turned into a complete mess. But, it would be a better and easier option to start from a better place. Most people function better when the home is in order and life is better organized. We feel more productive and a lot better. Maintaining an organized life and home takes a lot less effort when compared to starting from scratch all the time.

Interestingly, the key to having an organized home and life are the small daily habits that ensure the smooth running of your home, office and life generally. So, the focus of this section is on the extremely simple and small steps you can take, which over time will become habits. These are habits you can add to your habit stacking to form a routine which will make life better. Once you have made them habits, you need less attention and energy to maintain them. We shall start from habits that keep your home organized and gradually move on to habits that relate to your office and other aspects of life.

#1. Always make your bed every morning

This could take as little as 20 seconds but will instantly transform your bedroom and even help kickstart your proactive mood for the day. First thing you need to do every morning is to make your bed.

#2. Remove and fold your daily clothes

It's easy for neglected clothes to multiply and end up making the whole room cluttered. So, once you get home from work, change your clothes and fold, hang or put them into your laundry basket.

#3. Avoid putting anything on your couch

The only things you should allow on your couch are stylish blankets or pillows. Apart from these items, avoid putting other things on your couch. When the focal items (or big items) found in your room are clean, the entire room will look much more organized.

#4. Always clean as you go

You don't have to wait until you do a thorough spring cleaning; you will keep your counter or sink clean by simply wiping it with a kitchen rag. You can make crumbs disappear by using a mini vacuum cleaner.

#5. Maintain a small tray for your tiny essentials

One of the best ways to keep your home tidy is by having a small tray where you keep tiny daily essentials such as your wallet, ring, keys, etc.

Make it a habit of putting these items in the tray once you get home because it will save you the stress of rummaging through your home searching for your car or house keys in the morning when you're rushing to the office.

#6. Your dirty clothes should be kept in the laundry basket

Rather than leave your dirty clothes on the floor, bed or chair, place them in the laundry basket. It's often easier and better to have all your laundry in one place, rather than hunting for them every single time and possibly leaving some behind.

#7. Put everything back to its place

Well, if there is a golden rule of being organized, then this is it – having a proper place for all your properties. When your home items don't have a specific location where they are kept, they will end up lying around and causing clutter. So, as much as possible, designate a place for everything in your home and endeavor to put them back there as soon as you're done using them. This will just take a short time to become an automated habit.

#8. Eliminate digital clutter

Although digital clutter is less visible compared to physical clutter, it's still very annoying. Digital clutter makes it difficult for you to find your important files and also occupies so much valuable storage space in your desktop or laptop. Simply hit delete for all the files you no longer need.

#9. Keep your digital files in folders

Anytime you create a new document, try to instantly designate its place. You can either make a new folder or add it to the right folder.

#10. Always have a pen and notepad close to you

Have you wondered why you have several pens lying around in your home and you fail to find one when you need it? It's sometimes a mystery because most of us have experienced it severally, especially when you have kids at home. So, make it a habit to have a small notepad and a couple of pens close to your key tray all the time. This will help you whenever you want to jot down dates, daily tasks or the things you want to buy at the grocery store. Also, you can make use of your smartphone to do this.

#11. Update your calendar once you commit to something or an event

While it's possible for some people to keep all their commitments in their mind, there is a great chance that they can easily forget something. One vital organizing principle (especially for the working class) which gives you control is to update your calendar either on apps on your smartphone like Google calendar or your small notepad.

#12. Adopt the 2-minute rule

In simple terms, the 2-minute rule means that we should do everything we need to do that requires just two minutes or even less without delay.

Although this may appear to be a simple and small trick, it keeps you more productive and organized and prevents you from being faced with thousands of tiny tasks at the same time. Even though these tasks may be small and simple, they often leave you with much satisfaction after getting them done and this, in turn, gives you a huge productivity boost.

#13. Review your to-do list daily

At the end of the day, endeavor to review your to-do list to find out the tasks you have completed and the ones you haven't done yet. Cross out the tasks you've accomplished and plan for the next day with concrete action steps. Although this may take just five minutes, it will certainly keep you on track.

Chapter Nine
Career Habits

Every one of us are creatures of habits – we display a series of behaviors that take us through our day – from morning to night. Although these actions or habits aren't often well-considered, they are ingrained in us and influence our lives at home, in social settings and also in our place of work. Based on a study entitled "Habits - A Repeat Performance," which was conducted by David T. Neal, Jeffrey M. Quinn and Wendy Wood, it was determined that about 45 percent of our daily behaviors tend to be repeated in the same location on a daily basis. These habits are capable of either propelling us forward in our prospective fields and positions or hinder us too.

From the time we spend socializing on our smartphones and other devices to the websites we visit online, to our propensity for organization and productivity in the office and several other activities; career habits are actually a core indicator of our potential for success. These career habits below are essential for those who desire to succeed in their careers, excel at their jobs, and rise to the top of the popular corporate ladder.

Always Arrive Early - 30 Minutes Early

A good number of employees are late to work at least once each week, though there are more people who arrive on time. But, there isn't anything special about arriving just on time. Considering the highly competitive workplace, one career habit that you must adopt is to arrive early. When you arrive as early as 30 minutes before work time, you will have enough time to decompress and also plan your day. You will have enough time to create and execute a workplace morning routine, which will definitely give you an advantage of knowing what needs to be done for the day.

Keep your Workplace Organized

Probably, the leading career habit is organization. Apart from fostering a workplace that's clean and uncluttered, it helps increase the clarity of your mind. Clutter at first glance might appear disturbing to someone who is disorganized; it goes beyond that since it wreaks havoc on the subconscious mind. According to the results of a study which was carried out by the Princeton University Neuroscience Institute, it was revealed that:

"Multiple stimuli present in the visual field at the same time compete for neural representation by mutually suppressing their evoked activity throughout visual cortex, providing a neural correlate for the limited processing capacity of the visual system."

This implies that it's much harder to focus when we are disorganized since there are many things seriously competing for our attention. Since we are easily sidetracked, we often end up embracing the bad habit of checking social media or focusing on other activities that are not related to our work.

Make use of the 80/20 Rule

This is also known as the Pareto Principle which states that 80 percent of the results are achieved from 20 percent of the efforts. So, in sales, for instance, 80 percent of the sales a company makes are from 20 percent of their customers. You can leverage this principle in your workplace and focus more on the tasks that matter the most. Take some time to write down all the tasks you engage in and the outcome of the tasks. Identify where the 80 percent results from the 20 percent efforts come from and focus your efforts in those areas.

Add More Value

One of the hallmarks of the successful individual, organization or business is adding value to the world. It's impossible to move ahead if we fail to add value, so whatever you're doing, always endeavor at least initially to do the most amount of work for the least return. Well, most people might tend to do the least amount of work and expect the highest return, but that's not the best way to get ahead.

When you're adding value, people take notice of you. Your career will skyrocket when others see that you're doing the most amount of work in a bid to add exceeding value to your workplace. But always bear in mind that this won't happen overnight, but it will definitely happen.

Communicate Effectively

One of the key skills in the workplace is communication and individuals who possess this career habit (who communicate with their customers, managers, and colleagues) will always excel above others. So, you need to learn to communicate effectively by improving both your writing and speaking skills. What's the goal of communicating effectively? It will not only ensure that others understand what's on your mind, but it will also ensure that you understand and respond to the requests of others promptly. When miscommunication is involved, it's usually easy to experience disagreements, but these problems can be avoided when we communicate effectively.

Avoid Workplace Distractions

Considering the busy world we live in, you would agree with me that distractions are now like plague. We find ourselves wrapped up in them; smartwatches, smartphones, social media, etc. But what we need to do sometimes is to cancel noise and block out all forms of distractions in the workplace.

Practice Daily Gratitude in your Workplace

You should understand that the human mind tends to get what it focuses on. What this means is that when you focus on lack, you tend to experience more of it and on the other hand, when you focus on abundance, you get more of it as well. So, when you're always grateful, you increase the chances for abundance and also see things differently.

There are many things to be grateful for in our workplace and in life generally even though we easily get carried away by the problems we face. Every morning, spend 15 minutes writing down the things you are grateful for each day and you will gradually see as this career habit transforms your life by elevating your mood, improving your outlook on life and boosting your happiness.

Learn to Prioritize your day

The focus of this habit is on prioritizing your tasks each day. When you fail to list out and order the importance of tasks that you have to do each day, it becomes easy for you to veer off on a tangent. It's easy to overcome this problem by creating a to-do list and prioritizing it as well with effective time-management techniques. Your focus should mainly be on the tasks that can help you move toward your long-term career-related goals and at the same time, fulfill your short-term obligations in the organization where you work.

Show kindness to others

There is definitely no room for anger, hatred and resentment in the workplace and there isn't a replacement for being kind to other people. Strive to deal with any problem and move on; avoid dwelling on things. Regardless of who you may come across, it's impossible to know the kind of problems they may be facing in their lives. So, always have room for compassion and kindness. This doesn't involve you becoming a pushover, but it involves smiling and also taking an interest in other people. Try to spend time in knowing your colleagues at work, and talk about their lives, goals and show genuine interest in them.

Chapter Ten

Social Habits that Make you Likable

I believe that this is one of the sections that most people would love to read. One of the greatest mistaken beliefs is that being likable is natural and involves traits that are unteachable which only a few lucky individuals have – those who are good looking, the incredibly talented and extremely social persons. Well, it's possible that you also might have fallen prey to this misconception, but you shouldn't because being likable is something you can achieve. It's simply about emotional intelligence (EQ).

Based on a study which was conducted at UCLA, the subjects rated more than 500 adjectives based on their perceived significance to likeability. It was discovered that being intelligent, attractive or gregarious had nothing to do with the top-rated adjectives. Actually, among the top-rated adjectives include capacity for understanding someone else, transparency and sincerity. These and other adjectives described individuals who are skilled in the social side of emotional intelligence. So, what are some of the top behaviors that emotionally intelligent people engage in that make other people to like them?

1. They always ask questions

One of the greatest mistakes people make while listening is that they focus more on the next thing they are going to say or the impact of what the other person is saying to them that they fail to listen to what is being said. Even when the words are clear and loud, the real meaning is lost. You can easily avoid this mistake by asking lots of questions. It's one way to let people know that you are listening and that you care about what they are saying. You will be amazed at the level of respect and appreciation you will gain by merely asking questions.

2. Keep Your Phones in your pocket

Yes, nothing really turns people off during a conversation like a glance at your cell phone or a mid-conversation text message. Once you commit to a conversation, you need to focus your energy on the conversation. In fact, you will enjoy the conversation better when you immerse yourself in them.

3. Avoid Seeking Attention

People are easily turned off by those who desperately seek attention. Having an extroverted personality is not a good way to be likable. All that you need for people to be over you is by being friendly and considerate. People are usually more attentive and persuaded when you speak in a confident, concise and friendly manner than when you try to show that you're important. It's very easy for people to catch on to your attitude quickly and this means that they get more attracted to the right attitude.

Also, once you're given attention or recognized for an accomplishment, learn to shift the focus to those who worked hard to help you get there. If you do it genuinely, it will portray you as someone that's appreciative and humble. These are two adjectives that are closely linked to likeability.

4. They are Genuine

One of the essential qualities of being likable is being honest and genuine. No one really likes fake people and we easily move toward genuine people because we know that we can trust them. It's almost impossible to like people who you don't really know who they are. On the other hand, likable people generally understand who they are. These are people who are confident enough to be comfortable with their flaws. When you focus on the things that motivate you and make you happy, you will become someone that's very interesting. It's much better than making choices that you think will make people like you.

5. They are Consistent

If you're searching for one of the things that will easily make you unlikeable, then be the kind of person that's all over the place. People like to know who they're dealing with when they approach you. They like to know the kind of response they can expect from you. For you to be consistent, then you need to be reliable. Make sure that even in moments when your mood goes up or down, that it doesn't negatively influence the way you treat others.

6. They are not Judgmental

You need to be open-minded to be likable. When you are open-minded, you are approachable and others will find you interesting.

Generally, we don't like having a conversation with someone who has formed an opinion already and is not ready to listen to us. This habit is crucial, especially in the workplace where approachability implies access to help and new ideas. If you must erase all forms of preconceived notions and judgment, then you must see the world through the eyes of others.

Don't get me wrong; you don't necessarily have to believe what they believe or accept their behavior. What this implies is that you should avoid passing judgment long enough to understand their perspectives. This is the only way to get into their mind and understand who they are and what motivates them.

7. They Greet people by name

An essential aspect of your identity is your name and you often feel terrific whenever people use it. Likable people always ensure that they use the names of others whenever they see them. You don't have to use other people's name only when greeting them. According to research, people always feel validated when those they are communicating with refer to them by name. As much as possible, try to make remembering people's names an exercise. Don't be afraid to ask of someone's name the second time in case you forget it right after you heard it.

8. They make Positive Body Language

You can literally draw people to you like ants to a picnic by becoming cognizant with expressions, tone of voice (ensuring that they are positive), and gestures. Some forms of positive body language that most people with high emotional intelligence (EQ) use in drawing others in include uncrossing your arms, speaking with an enthusiastic tone, leaning toward the speaker and maintaining eye contact. You can transform a conversation by making a positive body language. Undoubtedly, how you say something can be more important than what you say.

9. They always Smile

Naturally, we tend to mirror the body language of those we are talking to. So, if you want your listeners to smile during a conversation, one of the things you can do is to smile at them and they will unconsciously return the favor and even enjoy the outcome.

10. Always Leaving a Strong First Impression

Available information from research indicates that people generally decide whether or not they like you within seven seconds of meeting you first. The rest of the conversation is then spent on justifying their initial reaction about you. Although this may be terrifying, you can also take advantage of this information now that you know to make outstanding gains in becoming likable. Generally, first impressions are connected intimately to positive body language. Smiling, a firm handshake, opening your shoulder to someone you're talking to and having a strong posture will ensure that you have an excellent first impression.

11. They know who to touch and touch them

Whenever you touch someone during a conversation, what you're doing is releasing oxytocin in their brain. This is a neurotransmitter which makes the brain associate you with not just trust but with several other positive feelings. A friendly handshake, a hug or even a simple touch on the shoulder is all that is needed to release oxytocin. Well, you need to be sure that you're touching the right person in the right way before oxytocin can be released.

This is because inappropriate or unwanted touching can actually have the opposite effect on people. Always bear in mind that relationships are built both by words and general feelings about each other and one excellent way to show care is by touching someone appropriately.

Now you have some of the habits of likable people. These are some of the things that make them invaluable and unique. Likeable people promote harmony in the workplace; they network with ease, often bring out the best in people around them and appear to have most fun. Once you add these habits to your routine, you will be amazed at how fast your likeability will soar.

Final Thoughts

We are all creatures of habits; they either empower us to achieve our goals or hinder us. Our habits can either make life more meaningful or terrible – depending on what we choose to do. We have been able to establish that the only way to eliminate unhealthy or negative habits is by replacing them with positive and healthy ones.

Well, the difference between your life before you picked up this book and now that you've finished reading it is what you do with the information. I can bet you that your life will remain unchanged and you will still get the same results if you decide to do nothing about what you've learned.

On the other hand, you can tremendously transform your life when you act on what you've learned. So, it's crucial that you take action now and begin to create habits stacks of the things you have learned. You can cultivate new and positive habits that will replace unwanted habits now. Hope you enjoyed reading and I look forward to a better and improved version of you!

Sources

Adams, R. L. (2017). 9 Essential Career Habits That Will Propel Your Success. Retrieved on August 22, 2019 from https://www.huffpost.com/entry/8-ways-to-supercharge-you_b_8080502

Baras, R. (2012). How to Change Habits: Habit Types and How they Form. Retrieved on August 21, 2019 from https://www.ronitbaras.com/emotional-intelligence/personal-development/how-to-change-habits-habit-types-and-how-they-form/

Bradberry, T. (2015). 13 Habits of Exceptionally Likeable People. Retrieved on August 22, 2019 from https://www.forbes.com/sites/travisbradberry/2015/01/27/13-habits-of-exceptionally-likeable-people/#35b0db7d1b14

Charles, D. (n.d). Life Potentials: The importance of good habits. Retrieved on August 21 from https://www.theworldcounts.com/life/potentials/the-importance-of-good-habits

Clear, J. (n.d). How to Break a Bad Habit and Replace It With a Good One. Retrieved on August 23, 2019 from https://jamesclear.com/how-to-break-a-bad-habit

Garfinkel, P. (2011). The 7 Habits Of Highly Spiritual People. Retrieved on August 21, 2019 from https://www.huffpost.com/entry/the-7-habits-of-highly-sp_b_78157

Gillikin, J. (n.d). Habits & Goal Setting. Retrieved on August 21, 2019 from https://smallbusiness.chron.com/habits-goal-setting-2508.html

Meier, J. D. (n.d). The Power of Habit Stacking. Retrieved on August 21, 2019 from http://sourcesofinsight.com/power-habit-stacking/

Ovenden, O. (2017). Habit Stacking: How To Train Your Brain With Routine> Retrieved on August 21, 2019 from https://www.esquire.com/uk/life/fitness-wellbeing/a15489/habit-stacking-chaining/

Rose, J. (2019). 27 Good Financial Habits You Need For Ultimate Financial Success. Retrieved on August 22, 2019 from https://www.goodfinancialcents.com/good-financial-habits/

Scott, S. J. (2019). 13 Steps for Building a Habit Stacking Routine. Retrieved on August 21, 2019 from https://www.developgoodhabits.com/building-habit-stacking-routine/

Viktoria. (2018). 15 Essential Daily Organizing Habits. Retrieved on August 22, 2019 from https://www.thelifestyle-files.com/15-essential-daily-organizing-habits/

www.ingramcontent.com/pod-product-compliance
Lightning Source LLC
Chambersburg PA
CBHW020613220526
45463CB00006B/2569